First Lesson
Clawhammer Banjo

by Dan Levenson

Audio Contents

1 Tuning notes - Key of G	24 Drop thumb - Example 12 - 1-2-1-5
2 Basic stroke - Example 2 - Brush thumb quarter notes	25 Drop thumb - Example 12 - 1-3-1-5
3 Basic stroke - Example 3 - Brush thumb eighth notes	26 Drop thumb - Example 12 - 1-4-1-5
4 Row, Row, Row Your Boat I	27 Drop thumb - Example 12 - 2-3-2-5
5 Chords in G - Example 4	28 Drop thumb - Example 12 - 2-4-2-5
6 Basic stroke chord exercise - Example 5, last line only	29 Drop thumb - Example 12 - 3-4-3-5
7 Row, Row, Row Your Boat II	30 Grub Springs
8 Little Brown Jug	31 Galax licks - Example 13
9 Cripple Creek	32 Breakin' Up Christmas
10 Finger to individual strings - Example 6, first string	33 Breakin' Up Christmas – Alternate A part
11 Finger to individual strings - Example 6, second string	34 June Apple
12 Finger to individual strings - Example 6, third string	35 Tuning notes - Key of D - double D tuning
13 Finger to individual strings - Example 6, fourth string	36 Chords in double D - Example 14
14 G scale	37 Double D chord double thumb exercise - Example 15
15 Mountain Dew	38 Double D chord drop thumb exercise - Example 16
16 Free Little Bird	39 Double Thumb D Scale - Example 17
17 Walking In My Sleep	40 Drop Thumb D Scale - Example 18
18 VII chord	41 Fly Around My Pretty Little Miss
19 Old Joe Clark	42 Walking in The Parlor
20 Hammer–ons - Example 9	43 Ducks On The Millpond
21 Pull–offs - Example 10	44 Tuning notes for G modal
22 Slides - Example 11	45 G Modal scale - example 19
23 Policeman	46 Shady Grove

1 2 3 4 5 6 7 8 9 0

Visit us on the Web at www.melbay.com — E-mail us at email@melbay.com.

Acknowledgments

There is no question that I could not do what I do without the heartfelt love and support of my wife and musical partner The Lovely Miss Jennifer Levenson.
She is a true inspiration and willing participant in our life of music and the road.

To my parents – long past – who taught and encouraged me to sing and play music from an early age.

I am thankful for all of you who believe in and support old time music. You have given me the opportunity to make it such a large part of my life as we share it together with the world.

Dan is endorsed by and endorses the following companies
It is through their work and support that I am able to continue bringing you this music.

Mel Bay Publications, Banjo Newsletter, Eastman Banjos,
Gold Tone Banjos, John Bowlin Banjos, Lee Banjos, OME Banjos, Vega/Deering Banjos,
Elixir Strings, Clifford Hardesty Fiddles, Elon Howe Fiddles, Red Diamond Mandolins,
Audio–Technica, The Stewart MacDonald Co. and Taylor Guitars.

Tablature has been set with *finale® 2012* software.

All sound tracks have been recorded with an Audio-Technica 2020 USB microphone
with a Bernunzio Music/Eastman Whyte Laydie style banjo
with Audacity® software which is copyright ©1999-2008 Audacity Team.
Web site: http://audacity.sourceforge.net/
It is free software distributed under the terms of the GNU General Public License.
The name Audacity® is a registered trademark of Dominic Mazzoni
Cover photo courtesy of the Deering Banjo Company

Table of Contents

Introduction – What's Clawhammer?   Starting at the beginning

Clawhammer is a banjo playing style that you find featured in at least two types of music. One is what we call *Old Time* and the other we'll call *Folk*. In today's old time music world, the banjo plays a co-lead with the fiddler and plays mostly fiddle tunes. And, though many of the older folks tell us that most if not all of these fiddle tunes once had words, the tune is the point and few complete songs are sung. The musicians in that style tend to get into one key and stay there playing tune after tune after tune for quite a while. Players also tend to retune their instruments for different keys, get into a key and stay there for a while (sometimes hours!) playing many tunes in that key in a group, or ensemble setting. This style doesn't have *leads, breaks* or *solos* and one person, usually the *alpha fiddler,* calls the tunes. It's a blast! That is the style that will be the focus of this book.

Then there is *Folk Banjo* (think Pete Seeger, Woody Guthrie and groups such as The Weavers, The Kingston Trio, The Limelighters and Peter, Paul and Mary, Folk songs and *hoots,* or *hootenannies*). There, the songs are king. The banjo plays the role of accompaniment instrument, somewhat like the guitar, playing chords and patterns to back up the singer – and the voice is the lead instrument. Pete Seeger was more of a singer who used a banjo to back up his singing instead of the other way around. If you are interested in that style, I would direct you to my book, *First Lessons Folk Banjo* (MB 22257).

Now that you understand some of the basic differences between styles, let's get you started on *Clawhammer Style* banjo playing so you can fit in and keep up in fiddle tune jams. We'll start out with some songs and tunes you may already know, then add the *bells and whistles* (as The Lovely Miss Jennifer likes to call them) that make old-time clawhammer banjo, well, *sing!*

The Banjo is sometimes called America's instrument. I like to call it a USA or United States Amalgamation because it has such an old and varied past, ending up today as a melting pot instrument of peoples and their cultures. The banjo is a member of the lute family, which traces its roots to Assyria – a country that no longer exists. Its ancestors (roots) come to us from many places, most notably Asia (China's sanxian, a skin-headed banjo type instrument said to date back over 4000 years), Africa and even Eastern Europe. If you want to see a vast representation of these instruments, I urge you to take a trip to the *Musical Instrument Museum* in Phoenix, AZ. It is a wonderful eye opening experience for this instrument and many others in our culture, and virtually every culture in the world and its music.

Today you can find all kinds of banjo things with 4, 5, 6 or even 8 or more strings. For this book and style, we are going to concentrate on the 5–string banjo. While in playing it matters little whether you have a resonator on your banjo or not (that wooden or metal cover on the back of the banjo), it just makes it louder and heavier. Socially, open back banjos are preferred for old time jams. They tend to have a more mellow sound than *resonator* instruments which are considered *bluegrass* instruments. So to fit in a bit better I recommend an open back instrument. You choose, but make sure it is a 5–string.

A NOTE ABOUT LONG NECK BANJOS - Pete Seeger is credited with the development of the *long neck* banjo. It is three frets longer than today's standard instrument, which allowed him to tune to the key of E. Unless *you* sing in the key of E as he did, I would recommend against it as a first banjo. It just adds weight, and you will have to capo-up right from the start to play with other musicians in the key of G. If you have one already, that's fine. Just be aware you will have to capo at the third fret for this book.

Parts of your banjo

Here are the basic parts of an open back banjo, which is the most common type (though not the only type) of instrument being used for old-time music today.

Headstock ---

Tuners (tuning keys, tuning pegs) --------------

Nut---

Frets---

Neck ---
Strings:

1-------------------

2--------------------

3------------------------

4---------------------------

5-----------------------------

Pot ----------------------------

Head ---------------------------

Bridge----------------------------

Tailpiece-----------

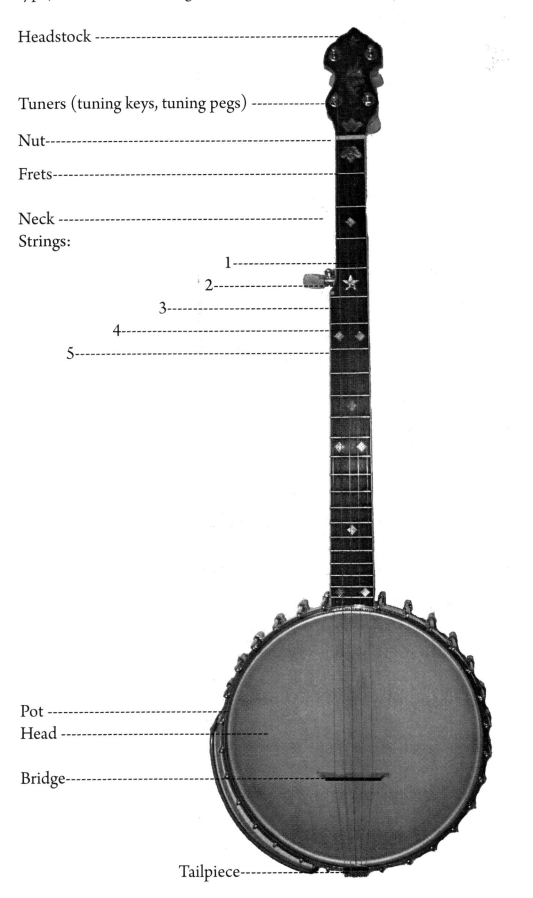

Reading tablature

This book is written in a type of music notation known as tablature. Reading tablature is in many ways easier than reading music. Tablature (tab) was developed to help you read music without actually reading music. Huh? Okay, tablature tells you where to place your finger to play a note on the banjo without actually having to know the note (A, B, C etc.). It does that by indicating what fret on which string you are supposed to put your finger to play a certain note.

In tablature, the lines of the staff indicate the strings of the banjo and the notes are numbers that tell you which fret number to put your finger on the string. The drawback of tablature is that it does NOT tell you which finger to use.

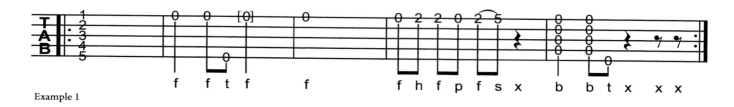

Example 1

In tablature (example 1 - above), the staff is the set of horizontal lines that the notes are written on. The word "TAB" tells you it is tablature. The two lines (*double bar*) with what looks like a colon next to it is a *repeat* sign. The beginning repeat has the colon to the right of the double bar and the ending one has the colon to the left of the double bar. They are used in pairs to indicate that you are supposed to play the phrase that is between them two times through before going on to the next phrase.

Banjo tablature has five horizontal lines per staff. The first measure shows which line represents which string. The "1" on the top line means that line represents the first string of your banjo and the "5" here tells you the bottom line is the 5th (short) string. This is just something that stays the same, so you won't see the string numbers on regular tab. (FYI, guitar tab would have 6 lines, mandolin tab - 4.)

The second measure shows the notes we use. A quarter note counts as 1 beat (say, "one"). Eighth notes count as 1/2 beat each so 2 eighth notes = one quarter note (say, "one and"), and a half note counts for 2 beats or 2 times a quarter note (say, "one, two"). The next measure shows a whole note, which counts as 4 beats (say, "one, two, three, four").

The fourth measure shows you a hammer on open string (0) to second fret (2), pull off from the second fret (2) to an open string, a slide from the second (2) to fifth (5) fret with a curved line above them (a *slur*) and a quarter note rest. (More on what these are later in the book). The final measure shows a quarter note, two eighth notes, a quarter note rest, two eighth rests and an ending repeat sign.

Notice the letters under the notes? The f and t indicate whether you use the finger - "f" or the thumb - "t" of your right hand to play the note. The "b" stands for brush across all the strings with your right hand's fingernail. An "x" indicates silence and means that you don't play this note.

The h, p and s give directions for your left hand. The "h" is a hammer-on, the "p" is for a pull-off and the "s" indicates a slide. These are all techniques you will be learning later in this book.

Holding your banjo

You know the song, She came from Alabama with a banjo on her KNEE - (not between her legs, right?) and my position is based upon this. When I sit, I like to hold the banjo on my right "knee" (thigh, actually) with the neck out to the left pointing out just below my shoulder (see photo). Some folks call this guitar style and I find this position to be the most natural and comfortable one for me. It is also about the same spot as the banjo hangs from a strap when I stand (see photo), so the bonus is that I don't have to change my playing position or style between sitting and standing.

Let's start here. I think you will find this comfortable as well. Even if you eventually choose another position, this is a good place to start. Like most things, there is no *right* way to do this. I will say that if what you do "hurts" (i.e. causes physical pain) then you may be doing something wrong. Other than that, you can try different things until you find the *right* one for you. BUT, for now, start this way.

Before we go any further, let's take a little time to get your banjo in tune.

Tuning your banjo

Clawhammer banjo players use different tunings for different keys. For our first tuning, we are going to tune to what is called G tuning. The notes you will tune your banjo to are gDGBD from the 5th string to the 1st. Remember the 5th string is the short one and the top one as you hold the banjo.

For many of you this may be your first stringed instrument and may even be the first instrument you have ever played. If you have played music before or even have experience with stringed instruments, this part should come easy, so forgive me if we take it a bit slow.

The notes in G tuning are gDGBD from the 5th (short string) to the 1st string. I have provided you reference pitches on the recording that comes with this book. (Tuning reference pitches Track...)

One very popular way to tune is with an electronic tuner. In this method of tuning, you will use the electronic tuner to tell you whether or not you are in tune and to what note. Basically, you play a string on your banjo into the tuner's microphone or you clip the tuner to your banjo directly. You can also use a pickup or tuning clip from the tuner attached to your banjo. The tuner electronically reads the note you played, tells you what note it reads, and how sharp (above) or flat (below) your note is compared to the note you want. Each tuner operates differently You will have to check the instructions that come with your tuner. Most tell you when you are in tune either by an in tune light, several lights, a centering needle or a combination of the two. They also have some way of telling you what note you have played. Like I said, check the instructions that come with the specific tuner you have.

There are also apps for your phone or iPod that can either read the note you play or generate a sound for the pitch you want so you can tune to it. They are quite handy and convenient, and many are free. I have several, but the latest from Peterson Strobe Tuners is the best one I have found. You can contact them at *www.petersontuners.com* for the most up to date info on this one.

Some tuners have trouble reading (hearing) a banjo's notes because of all the overtones (ringing sounds) from the banjo. This can cause you to get a false reading or sometimes even no reading at all from your tuner. Background noise from talking or other instruments can also make it hard for the tuner to pick out your banjo's note, which is why the tuning clip or direct attachment of the tuner to your banjo usually works better.

If you have not gotten an electronic tuner yet, you should try several before buying one. Take your banjo with you to do this. Check with friends, ask at the store you patronize, or specify to the order taker at the mail order place you deal with that you will be using this for a banjo. If the person you are talking to doesn't know which tuner to recommend, ask if anyone there does, and make sure you can return it if it doesn't work well with your banjo.

Because of the flexible head, banjo tuning is made more difficult since as you tune one string, others can go out of tune. To minimize this problem, I have a pattern I follow when tuning a banjo. Whether you tune to a pitch from the disc or choose to tune to an electronic tuner, tuning fork, piano or other instrument, I like to tune the strings in this order: 3 - 5 - 1 - 4 - 2 (tune the 3rd string first, then the 5th, and etc.).

Let's go back to the electronic tuner for now. First, start by playing the third string into the tuner and see what note the tuner says you have played. It should give you a name of the note it reads (i.e. A, B, C...) and an indication of whether the note you played is sharp ("#"- the note is too high) or flat ("b" - the note is too low). This string should be a G. Once you have gotten this G string in tune, go on to the 5th string. This is also a G note, only an octave (8 notes) higher, so you are again looking for the note to be G, and the in tune signal (light or needle) to tell you when you are in tune.

The next string I would tune is the first string. This should be a D. Next go to the 4th string D (yep, an octave below the first string) and finally the 2nd string - B. You can see we are crossing back and forth across the head while tuning. BUT, some movement has occurred so let's go back, start again, and fine tune the strings once more in the same order. Then, check them again one more time from 5 to 1 in order. The notes of your banjo strings should now match the reference notes on the CD. Now that we are in tune, let's start playing!

The basic stroke – double thumb

I hold my hand at about a 45-60 degree angle to the head of the banjo. My finger strikes the strings with the 10 o'clock position of the face of the fingernail. I use it somewhat like a guitar pick to strum the strings while my hand is going down towards the floor for the stroke (see photo).

I think of the hand as a unit, so as it strums down your finger strums (*brushes* or *strokes*) the four melody (long) strings, and the thumb should come to rest on (or just behind) the 5th (short) string. As your hand comes up it sounds the 5th string.

Let's go step by step. In the basic stroke, you are going to sound the 5th string every stroke. Don't worry when you start this process because you will often miss and hit another string or even no string. Just relax and think of keeping the hand together as a unit. I use my middle fingernail to strum the notes, but others prefer the index finger. Don't worry about which one to use. Just pick one for now. We call this *double thumbing*.

As your hand drops your finger sounds the melody strings (strings 4-1). At at the same time, the thumb lands on the fifth string. So, as your hand comes down for the strum for the first half of the beat, the thumb slips just behind (the head side of) the fifth string as in the photo.

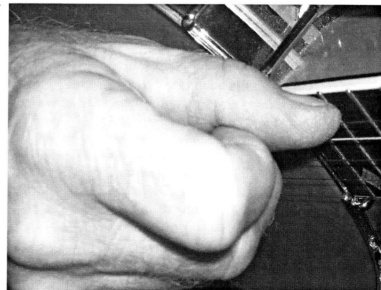

Next, you LIFT your *hand* and let the thumb *catch* the fifth string and sound it in a very natural way as your hand recovers back to the starting position. You may find it missing the string or not sounding it as you start working on this. Don't obsess over it, just get used to the gentle hand motion of stroking down with the fingernail and catching up with the thumb. Example 2 shows the basic stroke in tab with each stroke as one full beat. (Beat? Huh? Just a minute, first things first). Down–brush the strings, Up–5th string, hand recovers to the starting position. Drop/Lift/Drop/Lift ...repeat until smooth.

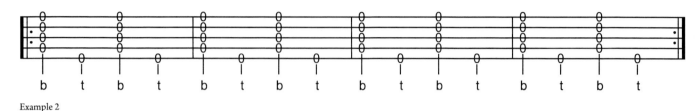

Example 2

Track 2

Remember—LET IT HAPPEN, DON'T MAKE IT HAPPEN

Timing and keeping time with a metronome

Okay, let's talk about the *beats*. Keeping time means playing your music evenly so other folks can stay with you. That means evenly counting time, which for most folks takes a bit of practice AND a guide. I don't mean tapping your foot here either. Keeping time is an acquired skill. In order to develop it you need a reliable source of the beat that is not influenced by your belief of being in time or any outside forces. Another way to say this is that if you can't keep time with your hands (yet), your foot doesn't do any better. What you need is called a metronome.

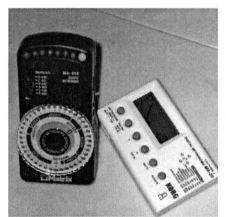

A *metronome* (photo left) is not a little urban up to date fancy dresser! It's a device that keeps time for you. It can be mechanical, requiring you to wind it up, or electronic - battery operated or plugged in. It makes a noise and/or blinks a light at regular intervals.

You set the time in the number of beats per minute (bpm) and then each click, beep or flash of the light counts as one beat. If you set the metronome for 100, the metronome will tick 100 times each minute. If you are playing quarter notes, you would play one note per click. If you are playing eighth notes, that would be 2 notes per click, etc. While it may SEEM like a Chinese torture device that is inflexible and unforgiving, a metronome will keep solid time for as long as you want! (Well, at least until the batteries run out or the spring winds down.)

The first thing folks discover when using a metronome is that you paid a lot of money for a device that doesn't seem to keep time any better than you do. BUT, after working with it for a while, you'll swear the darn thing figured out how you play and keeps time with *you*!

I know folks like to think that tapping the foot is an adequate substitute for a metronome. My experience and the studies of this method have shown that it does NOT work. Your foot tapping is controlled by your internal rhythm. Good internal rhythm is something that most folks need to develop and the metronome is the best way to get it. It's simple really:

If you can't keep time with your hand, your foot can't possibly be doing any better!

In addition, the foot can make a lot of noise and be pretty distracting especially when it is amplified by a microphone, stage and sound system. If you just gotta move something, try your head. Smile, bob and dance with your head, but play without tapping your foot.

Now, try exercise 2 again now with that ol' tippy tappy metronome counting time for you. Since it is quarter notes, each note gets one beat. This means that for each click of the metronome (you are using it right?) you get one beat and one direction of your hand. *Click 1* - hand down - strum the strings as the thumb lands on top of and just slips slightly behind the 5th string, *click 2* - the hand lifts and the thumb catches and sounds the 5th string as written in example 2. Cool huh? And no work, either. Remember to move from the wrist joint, not the elbow, finger or thumb.

Now, let's cut that in half. For the music we are playing to fit correctly, we have to divide each beat (quarter notes) into 2 half beats (eighth notes) so your hand can play both sides of the beat. This time for each click of the metronome the hand will go down AND up. For the first eighth note, the hand is now going to stroke down on the *downbeat* or the front of the beat and with the click. Then, you LIFT your *hand* and sound the thumb for the second part of the beat (that's right, the *upbeat* or *back beat*). In tab it looks like example 3.

Track 3

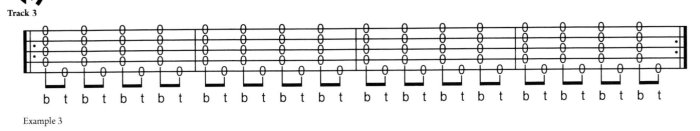

Example 3

It's time to play a tune! One you should know well from like, forever ago!

Row, Row, Row, Your Boat – I

Track 4

Key of G
G tuning – gDGBD

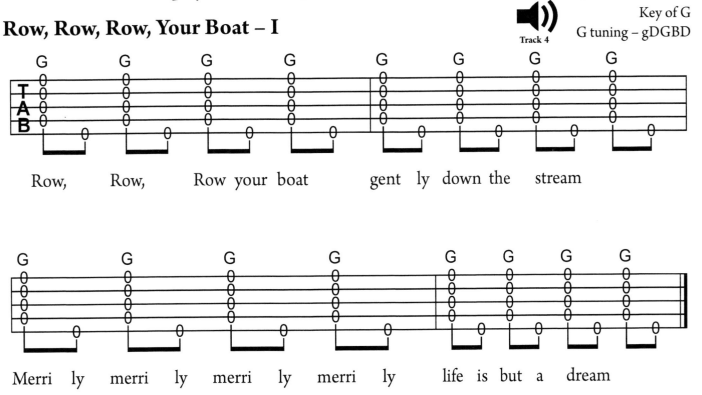

Say, did you notice that the last part of that tune didn't sound quite right?
Yes, that is because you were missing a *chord*. A what? A chord. "What's a chord" you ask? I'll tell ya!

Chords and fretting the notes

Webster's New World Dictionary defines a *chord* as "...a combination of three or more tones sounded together in harmony..." Without getting too technical, chords give you a very nice, full sound and are great for backing up a tune, especially if you want to accompany singing. Chords are comprised of a root, third and fifth of a particular scale played together. In the case of the of G chord, the notes would be G (root note of the G chord), a B (3rd note of the G chord), and D (5th note of the G chord). Played together, they make a full G chord. Hey! Those are the notes our banjo is tuned to right now! And that means you are ahead of the game right from the start! You already know and are playing your G chord. BUT, you are not done yet.

In order to play most basic tunes you need one or two more chords. If we consider the G chord the I (roman numeral I) chord, we need a IV and a V chord to get going further gently down the stream of playing old-time music with a banjo. And when I call them I, IV and V that means that they are the first, fourth and fifth chords of the scale. The key again is G, so G is the I chord. That means the other two chords for this key will be C (G, A, B, C – IV) and D (G, A, B, C, D – V). Well, the D chord is actually a D7 chord but lets not get into that now okay?

Your banjo is already tuned to a G chord – gDGBD. Put in chord terms, open 4th string (D – the 5th), open 3rd string (G – the root), open 2nd (B – the third) and the open first string (D – another 5th) and of course, our fifth string – g (another root).

Making the other chords – In order to play the other chords you need, you have to fret the strings – or press down the string near the fret – in order to change the pitch of each string to get the notes you want to make your chords. To do this, you place a finger of your left hand down on a string just behind (to the headstock side of) the fret (metal bar) for each note you want to play (see photo).

A student asks, "Which fingers do I use on my left hand to make the chords?" As I mentioned earlier, one drawback of tablature is that it tells you which fret to put your finger at, but not which finger to use. For now, I'll tell you. For the G chord, great news, no fingers down!

For the C – or IV chord, the tab shows a 2nd fret on the 1st string, a 1st fret on the 2nd string, an open (0) third string and a 2nd fret on the 4th string.

Start by placing your 1st finger at the 1st fret of the 2nd string, your 2nd finger at the 2nd fret of the 4th string and put your 3rd finger at the 2nd fret of the first string.

12

Start by using the tip of your finger for this as it is more accurate and you will need less pressure to get a clean note. As you can see in the photo on page 12, you have the neck of your banjo in your left hand parallel with the lifeline in that hand, and the thumb joint on the back of the neck just on or above the curve of the neck, pointing up (parallel or almost parallel to the frets). One way to get this is by making a circle with the finger and thumb, then put the banjo in place where the finger touches the thumb.

This allows you to curl your fingers so you can place your fingertip on the string just behind (the headstock side of) the metal fret. Press down only on the string you are fretting with only enough pressure to get a clear sounding note.

Too much pressure and you might notice your fingernail turning white. This will push the note out of tune, hurt your fingers and hasten the wear on your instrument's frets and fingerboard. Too little pressure and you will only get a dull, thuddy note.

Also, be sure to come down straight and clean on only ONE string or you will be deadening the one(s) next to it. The object here is to get a clean note on one string.

Try putting each finger down one at a time and sound it as a clear note before adding the next finger.

Once you have the whole C chord in place and all of the notes clear, let your right hand playing finger brush across all of the strings with the chord held down. Now lift your left hand fingers just a bit off the fingerboard and brush the open (G) chord, then put the fingers back down and brush the C chord, fingers off – G, on – C, off, on and etc. until you can just put the chord down clean and without watching your hand.

Now for your D7 – or V chord. Put the 1st finger on the 1st fret of the 2nd string, and the 2nd finger at the 2nd fret of the 3rd string. Repeat the process you did with the C chord of putting each finger down one at a time until you have a clean chord, then play with the chord, then without it, on, off, on, off (D7, G, D7, G) like before, until it is also clean and you can put the chord down without looking.

Example 4 shows each chord written in tablature with a standard fretboard diagram as well. Try strumming each one. (It's okay to let your thumb sound here even though it isn't written in.)

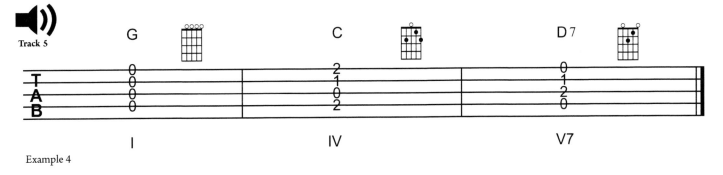

Example 4

HELPFUL HINT! If you only lift the fingers until they are off the string but still hovering over the fingerboard and strings, you won't get out of position with that one chord. This way, you won't have to travel far to change chords when it comes time to switch from one chord to another.

Here's an exercise so you can get comfortable with each chord, going from one chord to another, then through the entire I-IV-V or G-C-D7 pattern. This is what you will be doing for many of your tunes.

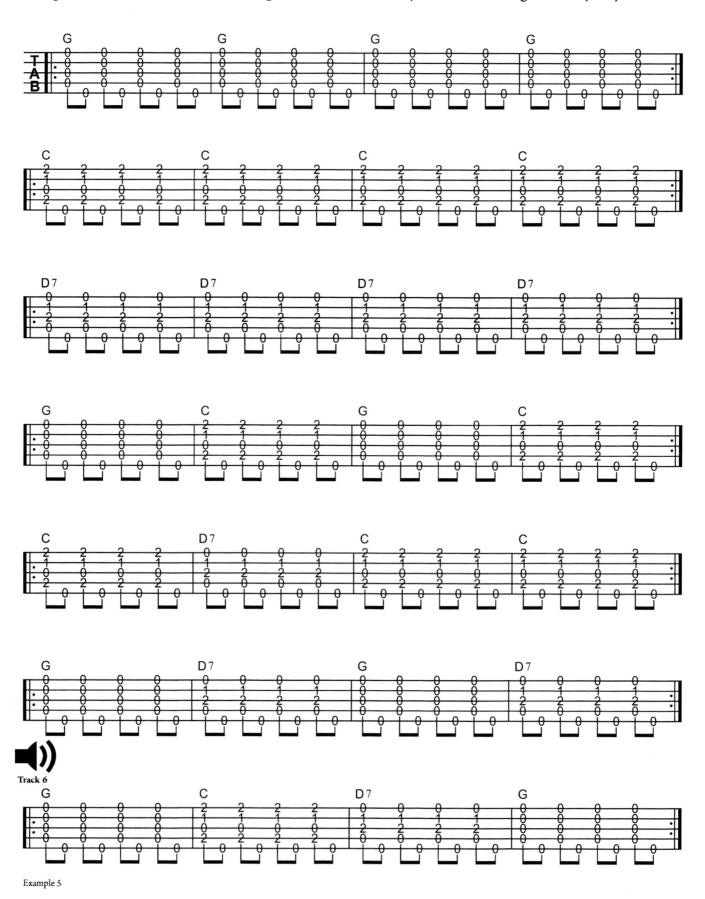

Example 5

These chord changes should all be smooth before continuing on to the tune.

Let's practice your chord changing with adding just one chord - the D7 (V7) chord at the end of *Row, Row, Row Your Boat.* Listen to how nice just this small addition of that one chord sounds.

Row, Row, Row, Your Boat – II

Track 7

Key of G
G tuning – gDGBD

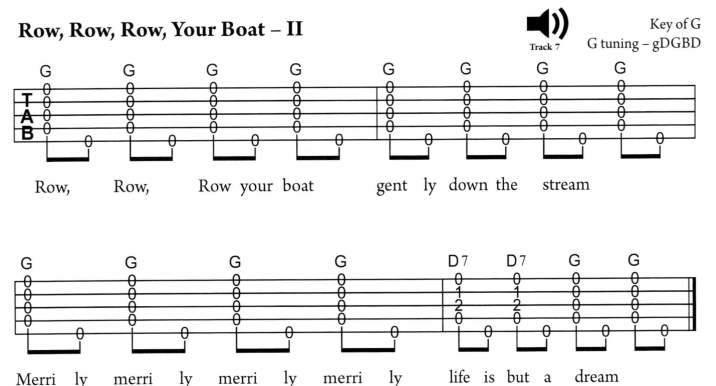

As you play it this time, here are questions you can be asking yourself as you work on this tune.

Are my arms and hands in a comfortable position? Are they where they go, or are they where I think they *should* be?

Is my thumb resting slightly pointed into (and somewhat behind) the fifth (short) string? Can I see the knuckle of my ring (third) finger?

Remember, I use my MIDDLE finger 'kauz it sounds bestest to me! BUT you get to choose! So, I bring the EDGE of my middle fingernail to the strings at about the 10 o'clock position looking at that nail.

Let the hand fall for the down beat strum (or brush stroke), then lift the hand to sound the thumb.

Repeat slowly enough to remember to put the D7 down at the word "life", but fast enough to sound like a song. Keep the flow and don't play too fast, but aim for not too slow either.

Starting speed–set your metronome at 50 and one full stroke/thumb per click. Brush on each click.

Ask yourself, "Are my wrists and hands relaxed, are my notes clean and the chord as clean sounding as the open strings? Do I notice ANY tension or the muddy notes, do I need to listen and relax more?"

You have done a great job today!
Good work here so you may just want to take a breather before adding the next step.

LET'S PLAY SOME MUSIC AND SING SOME SONGS!

SONGS? But Dan, you said we were going to learn tunes, what is with all the songs and words? Okay, okay, I'll explain. Before we can play tunes *note for note*, as the great old-time fiddle and banjo player Clyde Davenport once told me, you need some practice playing the stroke, changing chords and becoming comfortable with the basics. I find that words in songs give you something of an anchor to keep your beats together. By working with some songs that are familiar to most of you, it takes some of the pressure away and gives you that practice. So, a song or two to get you started. Some words, too!

Little Brown Jug

Chord changes with basic stroke and the original words from 1869!

Track 8 — Key of G
G tuning – gDGBD

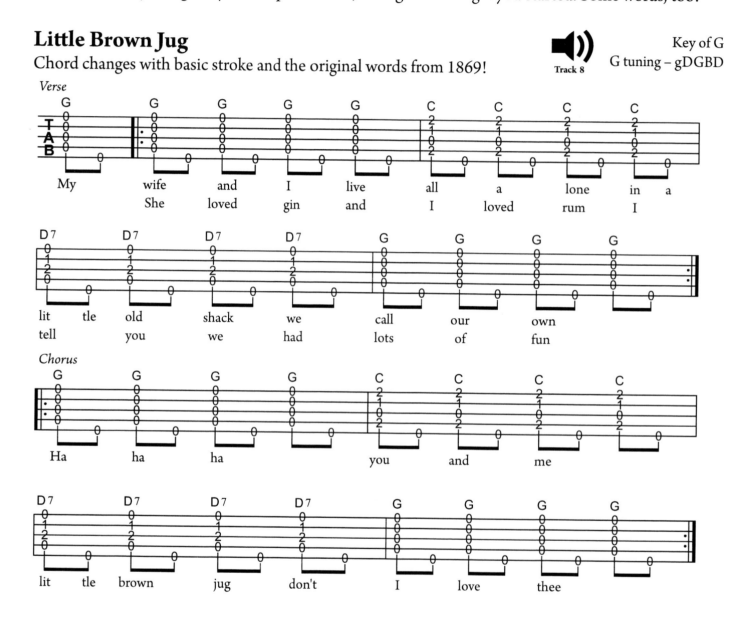

If I'd a cow that gave such milk, I'd clothe her in the finest silk;
I'd feed her on the choicest hay, And milk her forty times a day.

When I go toiling to my farm, I take little Brown Jug under my arm;
I place it under a shady tree, Little Brown Jug, 'tis you and me.

The rose is red, my nose is, too, The violet's blue, and so are you;
And yet I guess before I stop, We'd better take another drop.

Cripple Creek

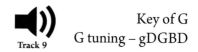
Verse

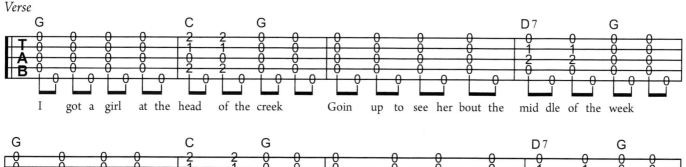

I got a girl at the head of the creek   Goin up to see her bout the mid dle of the week

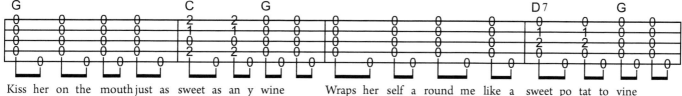

Kiss her on the mouth just as sweet as an y wine   Wraps her self a round me like a sweet po tat to vine

Chorus

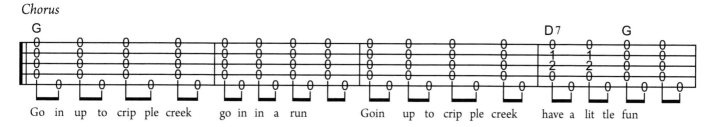

Go in up to crip ple creek   go in in a run   Goin up to crip ple creek   have a lit tle fun

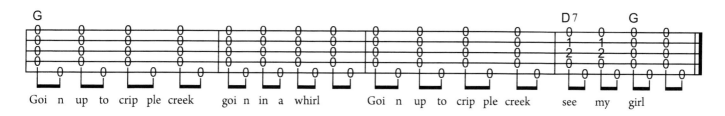

Goi n up to crip ple creek   goi n in a whirl   Goi n up to crip ple creek   see my girl

I got a girl at the head of the creek
Goin up t' see her 'bout the middle of the week
Kiss her on the mouth, just as sweet as any wine
Wraps herself around me like a sweet potato vine

Goin' up t' Cripple Creek, goin' on the run
Goin' up t' Cripple Creek t' have a little fun
Goin' up t' Cripple Creek, goin in a whirl
Goin' up t' Cripple Creek t' see my girl

Girls up on Cripple Creek about half grown
Jump on a man like a dog on a bone
I'll roll my britches up to my knees
An' wade in ol' Cripple Creek when I please

Goin' up t' Cripple Creek, goin' on the run
Goin' up t' Cripple Creek t' have a little fun
Goin' up t' Cripple Creek, goin in a whirl
Goin' up t' Cripple Creek see my girl

Let's find us some single notes!

While we can strum–thumb our way through almost any tune – and that is a good way to start learning a new one – if you want to *play* the tune, you have to start adding some *melody* notes. To do that your hand has to start to learn where each string is and make it sound by itself. In clawhammer playing this happens much the same way as we have been doing so far – we are just going to make it more accurate.

Here we go. You are already stroking down with your hand letting your finger brush over *all* the melody (long) strings, and letting your thumb catch to sound the fifth (short) string on the upward hand stroke, so you have the motion. Now I would like you to MISS (don't strike) all of the strings EXCEPT the first string (long one closest to the floor on your banjo) and only strike the first string with your fingernail as your hand makes its downstroke. Lift and sound the thumb. Once you get the first string clean, move on to the second string, then the third string, and then, yes the fourth string with your thumb sounding the fifth string after every *melody* note – i.e. the long strings which is where your *melody* for your tune is going to be played.

The example 6 shows a full line of each string for practice. Repeat each line until each string is clear and the notes are even. Once they are clean try going from one string to the next (ie. 1-2-3-4 and back again). You can do this with open strings (a G or I chord) or while making any other chord (your C - IV or D7 - V7) to hear how just changing a chord makes a difference in sound even without changing the exercise! Don't stress if you hit more than one string. Just keep working on it.

Finger to Individual Strings

Tracks 10 – 13

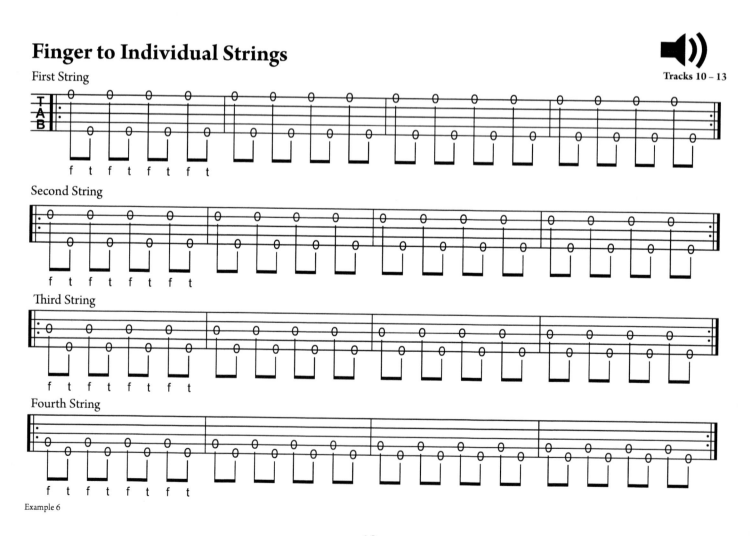

Example 6

One more piece here–The G Scale

Now that you can move from one string to another, you need to find the individual notes of the scale. Remember *Do–Re–Me*? It is those notes that make up the melody of the tunes you want to play. Here they are in tab with – you guessed it – the fifth string with every stroke. Yes, I know that it is beginning to sound monotonous and maybe even boring, but bear with me, we are almost ready to change that too! Here is a G scale in tab, and then we are going right into a song to put this into practice!

G Scale

Track 14

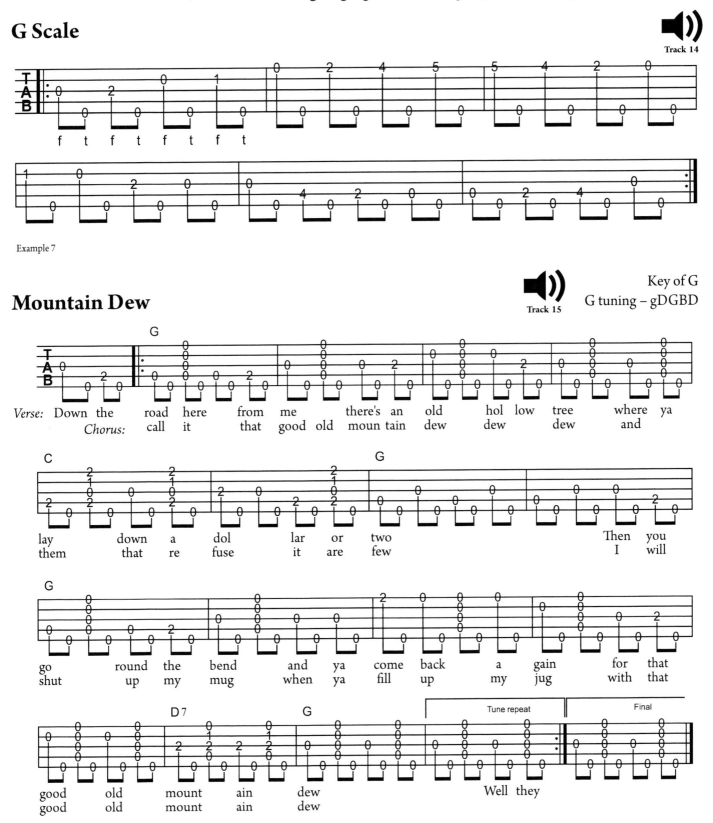

Example 7

Mountain Dew

Track 15

Key of G
G tuning – gDGBD

A basic rhythm - Pick/strum/thumb

This rhythm is often called the *Bum-Did-Dy* and it is what Pete Seeger called a *Basic Strum* and I call a *Basic Rhythm* or *Single Thumb*. It's kind of like the *boom–chuck–a* rhythm of guitar playing and it is comprised of a finger playing a single note, followed by a strum of the chord, then a thumb pluck. This doesn't change your two part hand motion, down and up but now, where the down stroke hits a single string on the first down of your hand, thumb hits the fifth string but stays SILENT (or almost silent) as you lift your hand. Then you stroke a single string or brush a chord with your finger on the next downward stroke of your hand, this time letting your thumb catch and sound as you lift your hand. Don't worry if your thumb sounds when you don't want it to and/or doesn't sound when you do. Variety is the spice of banjo and practice will allow you to get the sounds when you want them and not get sound when you don't. It will come.

Rather than another exercise, I think we can go right to a tune and combine the bits. It is when you mix the finger strike on melody notes and follow it with a strum thumb that the tune starts to become musical and some of these little exercises start to make sense. Also, when you start to vary or use a different string for the single note, things REALLY start to change. SO,

It's tune time...

Free Little Bird

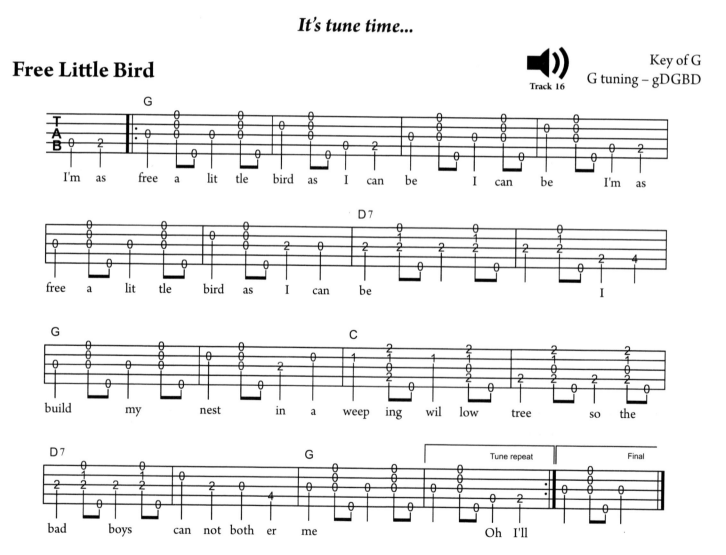

You are REALLY starting to get this! Let's take another step and put ALL of our techniques together.

This next tune combines everything we have worked on so far. There are brush thumb strokes but some of them are only partial chords because you don't always hit all four strings, sometimes only two or three. You don't need to be too careful here. If you catch all four strings, fine, if only 2 when three are marked, that's okay too.

There are also lots of single notes both in our double thumb (finger to a *melody* note, thumb to the 5th string), then there are our *basic rhythm* quarter note–eighth–eighth where the thumb stays quiet–or mostly so. If it sounds sometimes when it's not written, ok, if it doesn't sound when it is written, that's okay too! Just make sure your hand is working as a unit. Down–up–down–up–finger–thumb–brush–thumb–f–t–f–t...AHA! See the markings under the notes? Now instead of words, you are starting to get the right hand directions. Remember f = finger, t = thumb and b = brush.

Two more things. A part/B part - most fiddle tunes have two parts. Each is played two times (see the repeat signs?). If both endings are the same, you just get the repeat sign, but if the two endings are different, you play the one marked *1* for the first time through and the one marked *2* for the next time.

Walking in My Sleep

Track 17

Key of G
G tuning – gDGBD

The Capo and other keys

Capo – there was once an amusing booklet on clawhammer banjo playing that said, *a capo is that device that allows a banjo out of tune in one key to be instantly out of tune in any other key.* (Doc Stock Banjo Method). While that sounds funny on the face of it, it is not far from the truth. A capo is a mechanical finger or clamp that holds all of the melody strings (1st to 4th strings) down at the same time at the same fret, which then lets you change keys without having to retune your banjo.

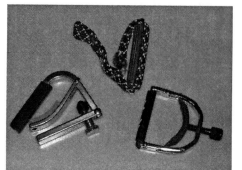

There are a many good capos on the market. Most of them (Schubb, Kyser, Paige and G7 to name only a few) are very easy to use, protect the instrument and give even and accurate pressure for around $25–$30. I would warn you against the cheap elastic ones because they are cumbersome, not very accurate, and the rivets in the strap tend to severely scratch the banjo's neck.

To use the capo, put it on the neck just behind or on the headstock side of the fret you want to capo. There are several different designs of capos so you will have to check the instructions that came with yours to see how it works (spring clamp, screw setting, etc.), but they all do the same thing even if they do it in different ways. This changes the key of your banjo in half steps according to the fret you are capoed at.

Each fret is a half step, so if your four open strings are tuned for G tuning (4-1 DGBD) and you put the capo at the first fret, you bring the banjo up to G# - or one half step. Go to the second fret and you are now in A. Your capoed strings are now EAC#E (4th to 1st strings) and you are now ALMOST in the key of A. Why almost? Because you still have to deal with the fifth (short) string.

While the main capo clamps on the first four strings, you still need to retune the 5th string up the same number of half steps (each fret = 1/2 step up the musical scale) as you did with the capo. The easiest way is to just retune the fifth string to match the NEW fifth fret on the first string. SO, if you capoed up 2 frets to the key of A, then you would retune the fifth string to *a* also. BUT this only works up to a point. Above that *a* the string will most likely break so we need another alternative if you want to capo more than two frets up from the key of G.

Permanently mounted 5th string capo

You can get a 5th string capo which works much like the capo described above, except that it only hits the 5th string and is permanently installed on the banjo, or *spikes* – actually small HO railroad spikes which allow you to slip the 5th string under them acting like a capo (see photos).

Both of these items should be installed for you by a competent luthier familiar with banjo spikes and fifth string capos. Or, you can make a quick and handy one from a stick pen cap like in the photo to the right!

5th string under *spike*

Home made 5th string capo

Once you are all tuned up, the notes of your strings will now be tuned *aEAC#E,* which puts you in the key of A. Your old 2nd fret is now your new nut, so you have to count up to the new 2nd fret NOT counting the one where the capo is your old 4th fret (i.e. the seventh fret without the capo becomes the new fifth fret). SO, the tab numbers refer to the fret number after the one the where capo is placed.

The finger positions of your I, IV, and V chords when you are capoed up are exactly the same. Only the names changed one full musical step up, so the G is now A, C is D and D is E. (I-IV-V starts to make sense, eh?) You can change to other keys too by simply moving the capo, adjusting the 5th string and using the same I–IV–V positions.

The VII Chord

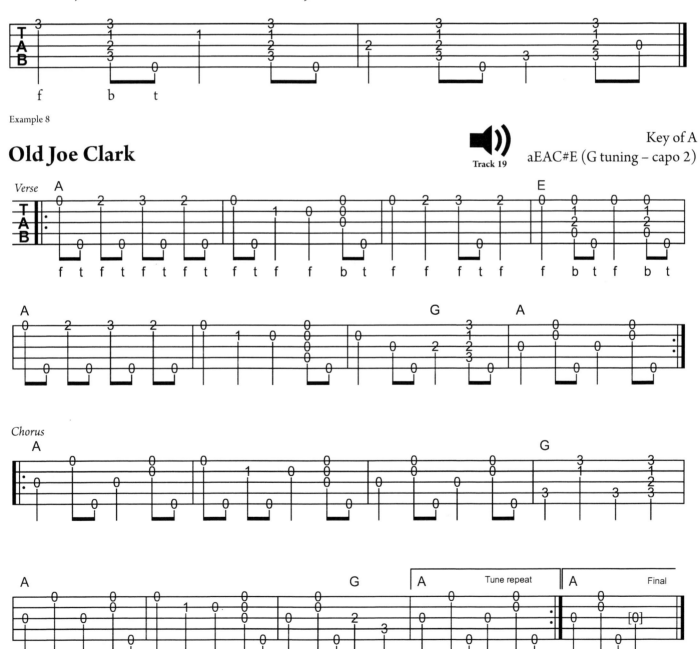

The *VII* chord refers to the 7th chord of the key, so since we are in A the VII chord is a G (A-B-C-D-E-F-G). (In G the VII chord would be F). The VII chord appears in many A tunes these days, so we'll just pop it in here for that old-timey sound. Here is the chord in tab using the basic rhythm stroke while moving the single string melody note from string to string (yes, the 5th string does sound funny with this chord.) Next we'll use it in the tune *Old Joe Clark*:

Example 8

Old Joe Clark

Track 19

Key of A
aEAC#E (G tuning – capo 2)

23

Hammer–ons, pull–offs and slides

We'll stay in A for this exercise. Up until now, the only way you have played the second half of a beat is after the strum with the thumb, and *that* was always an open 5th string. These next techniques give you a nice introduction into more advanced tune playing and are what Miss Jennifer often calls, *the important bells and whistles* that make banjo playing so dynamic. They also let you get a few more notes in when playing a tune!

Hammer-On – A *hammer-on* occurs when you place a left hand finger down on a string hard enough to hear the note sound. It can be to a fret from an open string or another fret up the scale from an already fretted string. Here are three hammer-ons tabbed out for you in example 9.

Track 20

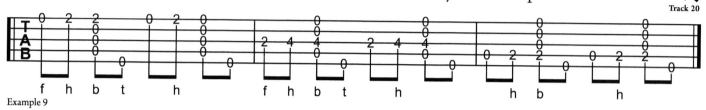

Example 9

(*Note: I put all of the right and left hand notations under the first measure to start then gradually reduce the notations to only the ones you should need*).

Pull-Off – A *pull-off* is sometimes called *left hand pizzicato* and involves plucking a string with a *left* hand finger as you *pull-off* of one note to a fret below (a lower note on the scale) or open string. Here are three different pull-offs in tab in example 10.

Track 21

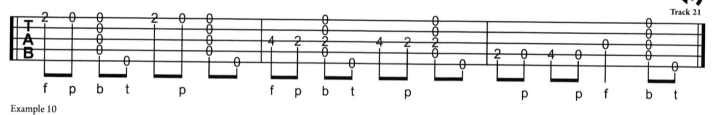

Example 10

Slide – A *slide* occurs when you move your finger from one fretted note to another fret up OR down the scale without fully lifting it off the fingerboard as you *slide* from one note to the other. Notice the curved line above the notes of the slide. That is called a *slur*. Some folks also put a slur over hammers and pulls, but I only put them on slides because they indicate a continuous tone from start to finish of the slide whereas hammer-ons and pull-offs are made up of two seperate notes or tones. Here are three types of slides written out for you in example 11.

Track 22

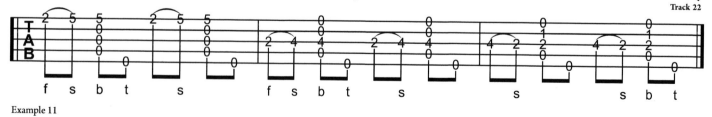

Example 11

We are going to put these to work right away in a very popular A tune – *Policeman*. This one is a core tune in the old time repertoire and often played at jam sessions around the country.

Policeman

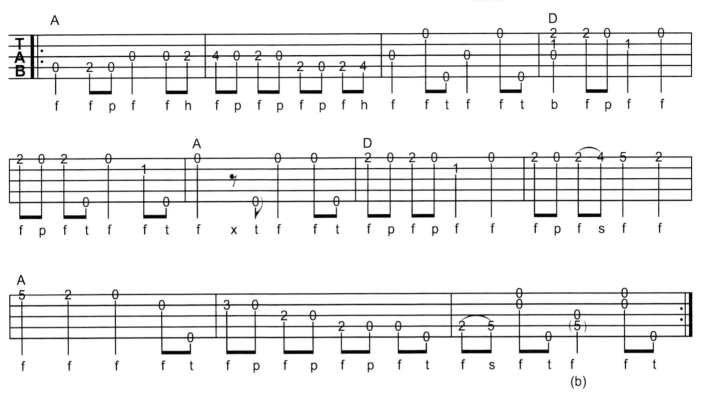

Police come to my back door this morning; Police come to my back door this morning;
Police come – I didn't want to go; Tell 'em I don't live here no more this morning...

Notice that this time I put all of the right hand directions under each note. Yes, even though you perform hammer–ons, pull–offs and slides with the left hand, they are called right hand directions because they actually tell your right hand that the left hand is going to perform them! Confusing, I know, but that's why it's there. Remember, your right hand still lifts as though the 5th string were going to sound, even though it doesn't for those h, p, and s's (okay, yes, it can if you like).

Next, you will notice there is an *x* in the second line, second measure under the rest (that little squiggly thing) where you would have normally hit a fingered note with your down stroke. This time you miss or *skip* the DOWN note which makes a very nice syncopation. No, no one will be upset if you hit a note here, but it is cool to have that little hiccup in the tune. You'll be using it again someday.

And finally, in the last line, last measure, do you see the 5 and *b* under it in parenthasis ( ) below the 0? That is my way of telling you that note is optional. See where you slide from the second fret up to the 5th at the beginning of that measure? Well, that 5th fret on the 4th string and the open 3rd string are actually the same note. If you hit both, it becomes a brush stroke as indicated by the *b*. So, you can hit that string *and* the open 3rd string together which will sound fuller, but you don't have to. Your choice. Try it both ways. You can do it sometimes and not others too!

WOW, you have really worked hard! I do know you are making great progress and having fun too.

I only have just a few more techniques I want to teach you. The next one is called *Drop Thumb*. Some folks consider it to be the most important skill that makes this style so unique.

Drop Thumb

The term *drop thumb* refers to the action of playing an inner or *melody* string with the thumb. This allows you to play more of the melody of a tune when the melody notes fall on the second half of the beat – just like your hammer–ons, pull–offs and slides. It also adds more rhythmic variation and texture. Though there are exceptions, the thumb almost never plays the same string you played with your finger or a string below the fingered string (i.e. finger plays the second string followed by a thumb to the first string). The hand still drops and lifts, but the thumb passes by the fifth string going instead to any other string. So, when you bring your hand down in the first line, the finger still strikes the first string, but the thumb aims the hand towards and catches on the second string, which will sound as you lift your hand. Here is an exercise to cover most possibilities and combinations.

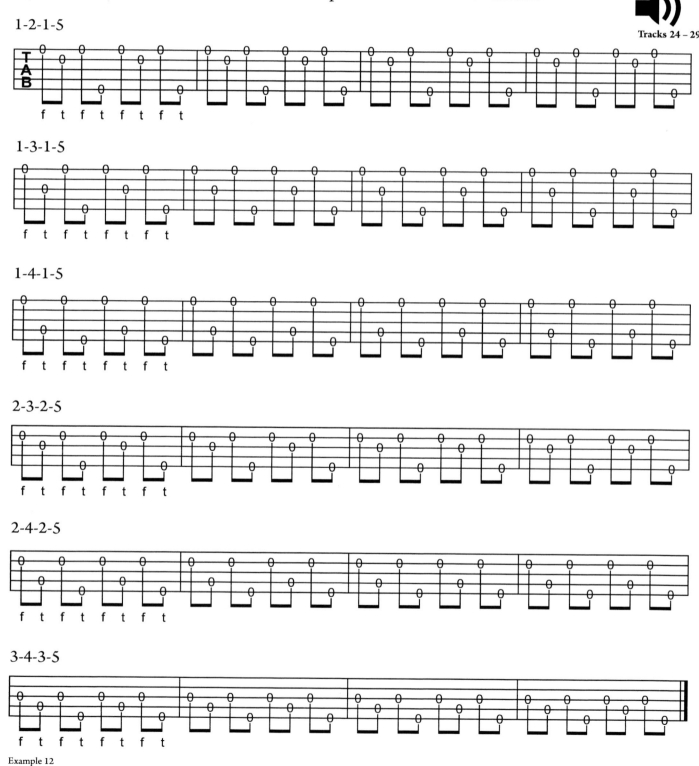

Tracks 24 – 29

Example 12

26

Grub Springs

A part

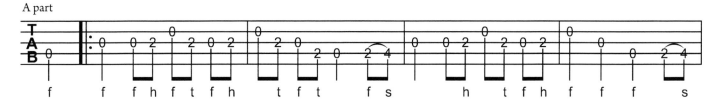

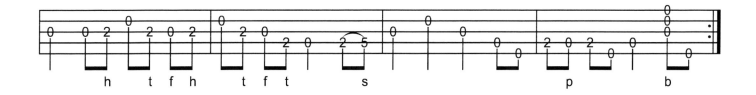

B part

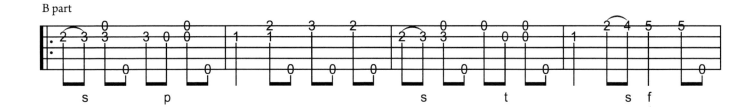

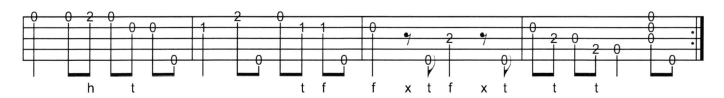

This is one of my favorite A tunes. You can have a lot of fun with this one. It is full of drop thumbs, hammer–ons, pull–offs, slides and SO much more. The rests near the end add to the syncopation.

I've marked all of the drop thumbs, hammers, pulls, slides and more, but not every finger strike. If you find you have a question as to whether or not to use a finger, thumb or something else, there are a couple of good rules to help guide you.

If the note is at the front of the beat (usually a quarter note or first of two eighth notes) it is most likely played with the finger as your hand is stroking down. If it is on the back (second half) of the beat - such as the second eighth note in a pair, it is probably a thumb, hammer, pull or slide.

If that note goes up the scale, it is most likely a slide up or hammer–on.

If that note goes down the scale, it is most likely a pull off, slide down or a drop thumb note.

Yes, there are exceptions to these. You *can* pull–off of a string that has not been sounded by the finger and you *can* hammer–on to a string that has not been sounded. These are called alternate *string pull–offs* and yep, *alternate string hammer–ons,* but these are not used often. I won't do that to you in this book. Promise! Next we'll introduce the *galax lick* then give you a couple tunes to play it on.

Introducing the *Galax Lick*

Track 31

This *lick* involves playing two notes (or a *triplet* – 3 notes in the space of 2) in a full beat length downstroke with your hand. THEN a full beat thumb note played on the 5th string as your hand comes up on the next beat. One or two 5th strings with the thumb. Here are 3 common galax licks.

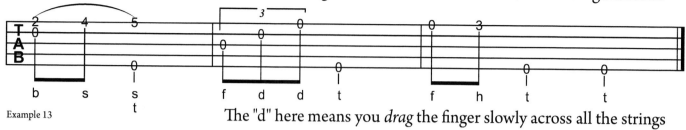

Example 13

The "d" here means you *drag* the finger slowly across all the strings

Notice the tune has an alternate A parts. Use one or the other or mix them up. Lots of fun stuff here!

Breakin' Up Christmas

Track 32

Key of A
aEAC#E (G tuning – capo 2)

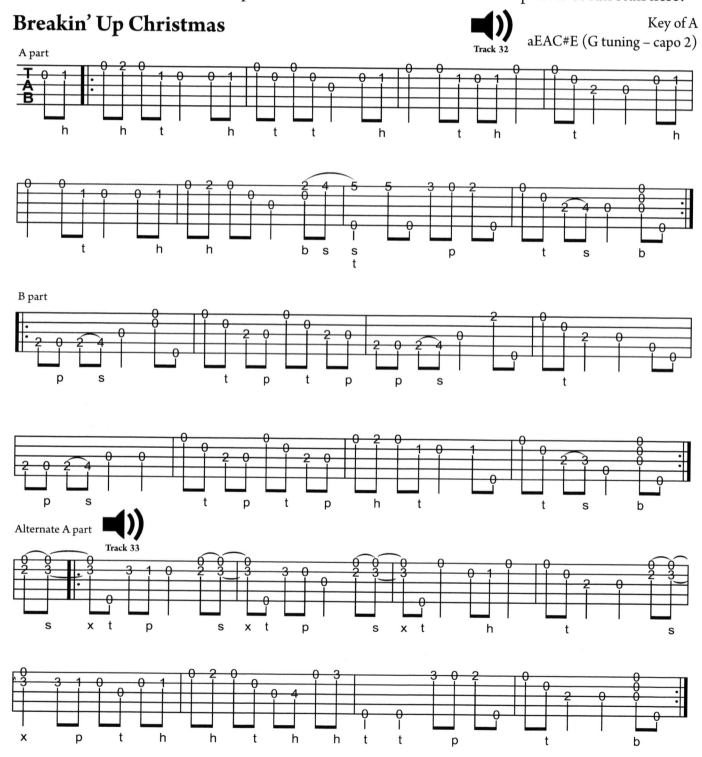

June Apple

Key of A
aEAC#E (G tuning – capo 2)

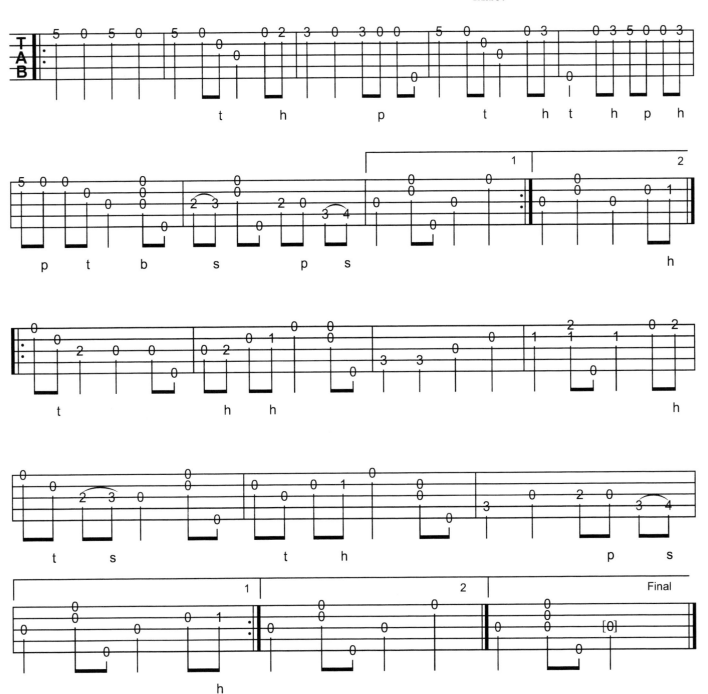

These words fit the second part. Call 'em out now and then and you'll be stylin'!

Wish I was a June apple, hangin on a tree. Everytime my gal walks by, take a little bite of me.
Wish I had a nickle, wish I had a dime. Wish I had a pretty little gal, I could call her mine.

Nothing really new in this one. Another jam regular and favorite tune of the old-time set, me included. Did you notice the galax lick at the end of the fourth measure?

Say, you are getting pretty good here in this tuning. Time to show you another one!

The Key of D or *Why do those folks stay in one key for so long?*

Here we go, time to move out of the comfort zone of G tuning. Even when we went to the key of A the relative tuning of the strings and chord figures didn't change. In fact, for the folk and bluegrass crowd, one tuning and a capo is all you need for many keys. Sure, some do change tunings, but most folks playing in those traditions don't tend to retune their instrument much. I think it was John Prine who once said that if not for the capo, all of his tunes would be in the same key. Doc Watson called it his *hillbilly crutch*. No, I'm not disparaging the capo; it's a very useful tool. But, we do it differently.

The old time banjo and fiddle players tend to retune their instruments to match the key they are playing in. Why? Well, tradition can be blamed for some of this (*that's the way my daddy did it*), lack of formal musical training could be another reason, but the best reason for me is that retuning the instrument allows you to play notes in one tuning that might not be easily playable in another. And, it sounds different! While there is historical precedent even in classical music for retuning the instrument (the *proper* term is *scordatura* – literally translated as *mistuning*) it is mostly kept alive in this type of music. Because of this retuning, old time jam sessions tend to get into a key and stay there for a long time. Hey, ask yourself, do *you* want to retune your banjo for every other tune? I don't either...

In old time music, the key a tune is played in is usually governed by the key that the fiddler plays it in. For all of the same reasons I mentioned, each tune has a key most fiddlers play it in. I have found the most common key in old time music is D. That is, there seems to be more tunes – especially the more common jam tunes – in D than any other key. So that is where we are going to go next.

If you are still capoed to A, I suggest taking the capo off and going back to G for ease of tuning. Trying to tune with the capo on just makes it harder because the strings won't move easily due to the pressure on them.

The tuning we are going to end up at is often called *double D* (or *double C* without the capo) to distinquish it from *standard C* or *old C* tuning, which are not often used these days.
The notes for double D are:

aDADE
Track 35

Tuning is easier without a capo on the strings. SO, first, take your capo to get back to G tuning (gDBGD). (You can leave your fifth string tuned up to a if you like. We'll be going right back there). Now we tune the banjo to double C (***gCGCD***) by doing the following:

> 1– Tune your second string *up* 1/2 step from B to C
> 2 – Tune your fourth string *down* 1 whole step from D to C

You are now in *double C* and tuned gCGCD

Next:
> 3 – Put your capo back on at the second fret
> 4 – If you have tuned your fifth string down, capo or spike the fifth string (remember, that's the short one) up two frets or tune it back up to *a*.

That's it! You've done it. Your notes in double D are aDADE and should match the pitches on the disc.

Chords and scales in D

All we need now are some new chords and a new scale to get you familiar with the notes in D which I have tabbed out for you on this page. I have given you double thumb chord exercise to get you started playing and changing the new chords. This will give your hand a good anchor in this tuning.

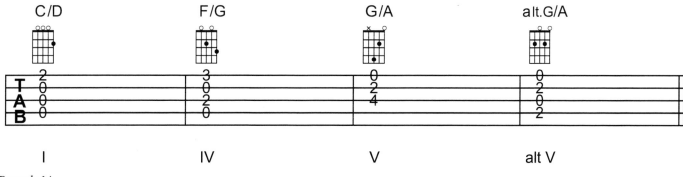

Example 14

Here are our chords - I, IV, V and another one - the alternate (alt.) V chord. I have listed their names for each key. If we were in C they would be C, F and G; when we are in D, they are D, G and A. The chord shapes (fingering and hand positions) stay the same in both keys as shown by the fingerboard diagrams. (I, IV, V is starting to make some sense, no?)

The fingering: **I** - Put your index finger at the 2nd fret of the first string. All the other strings are open. **II** - Index finger at the 2nd fret on the third string, third finger at the 3rd fret on the first string. Second and fourth strings are open. **V** - New ground! See the "x" above the 4th string in the chord diagram and no note on the 4th string in the tab? That means you don't play that string because that note is not part of the chord. If you do play it (and many do) just chock it up to banjo sound, no one will hurt you. So, you use the index finger at the 2nd fret of the second string, the third finger at the 4th fret of the third string, and an open first string. **alt. V** – This one can be a bit awkward. Use either the index finger, 2nd fret on the fourth string and your middle finger, 2nd fret of the second string, OR middle finger 2nd fret on the fourth string and third finger 2nd fret on the second string. The other strings are open.

Fortunately these are easier to do than they are to read about! Here's a simple double thumb chord changing exercise. As always, make this smooth and steady before moving on. Feel free to rearrange the chords in different orders to make your own exercise version.

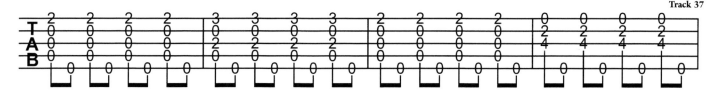

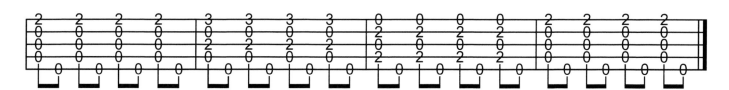

Example 15

31

Next, a drop thumb version of the chord exercise. It may seem tricky, but if you put your chord position down first, you just play your old drop thumb pattern as 1–2–brush–5.

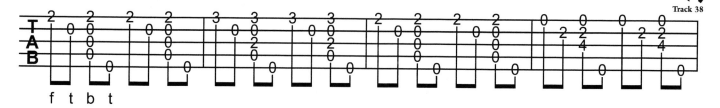

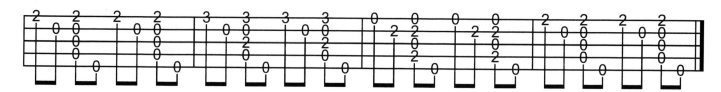

Example 16

Now for that scale. Double D tuning (aDADE -double C capo - 2), double thumb pattern first. I've added something for this scale. One time only. Left hand fingering! Why? Because I think in this tuning it is especially important to use your left hand efficiently. To do that I start by using my index finger at the second fret and then each next finger for each next fret on the string. Also, when you get up above the fifth fret – as you do on the first string – I thought it only fair to tell you how to get there. Pretty straight forward – i = index finger, m = middle, r = ring and p = pinky. Yeah, you can do it!

Track 39

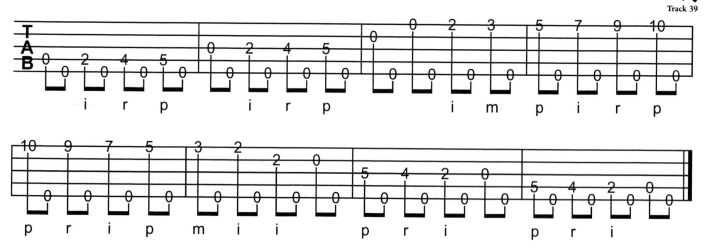

Example 17

Finally, the double D scale with a drop thumb pattern that will almost make it seem like it is a tune!

Track 40

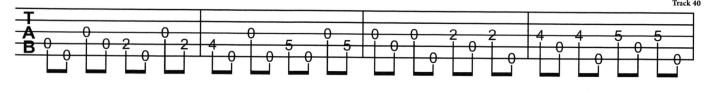

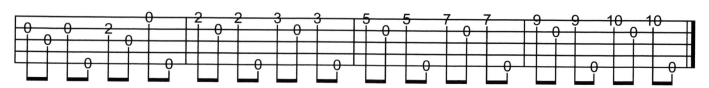

Example 18

SO–HOW ABOUT A TUNE?!?! (Yes, in D)

Fly Around My Pretty Little Miss
aka Western Country; Susananna Gal

Track 41

Key of D
aDADE (double C tuning – capo 2)

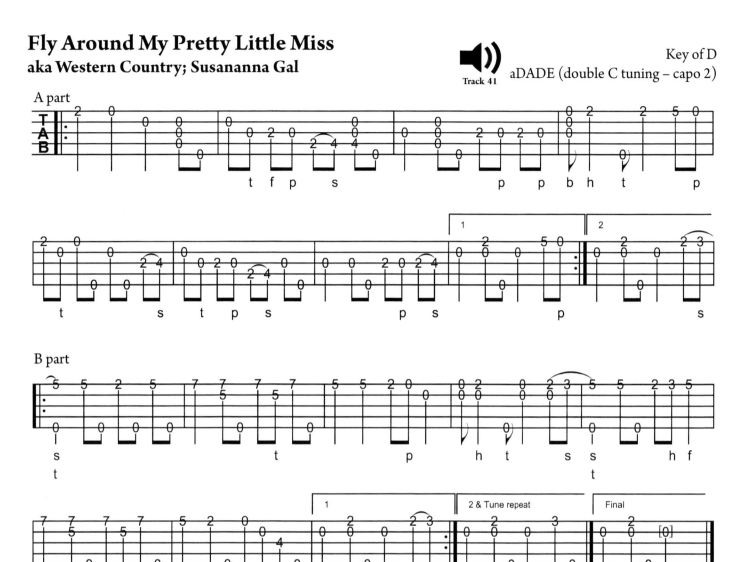

Fly around my pretty little miss, fly around my daisy,
Fly around my blue eyed gal, you almost drive me crazy.

I'm going to the western country now, Susananna gal.
I'm going to the western country now, Susananna gal.

How do you make your livin', Susananna gal?
By drinkin' whiskey and playin' cards, Susananna gal.

Hitch ya a morgan in the front, morgan in behind,
I'm goin' down that rocky road, I'm goin' see that gal of mine.

If I had no horse to ride, I'd be found a'walking,
Up and down old toenail gap, hear my boot heals talkin'

Walking in The Parlor

Key of D
aDADE (double C tuning – capo 2)

You'll have some fun with this one! Hammers, pulls, drop thumbs and a bunch of syncopation.

The way this is written out, there are no repeats for each part. Play the tune straight through using the *Tune repeat* measure to go back to the beginning and the *Final* measure to end the tune.

See the last measure of the first line? You play this by brushing the open strings, hammering your first finger onto the second fret of the 1st string, and then holding that note into the next measure. That x under the first note of the second line means you let the notes continue to sound without hitting them again. It happens again in the B part, then again as you repeat the tune.

This version is based on the 1926 recording by The Hill Billies. The Highwoods String Band recorded it later in the early 1970s on their Fire on the Mountain LP (now available as download). You will find the first part a bit different from the Wade Ward version in my Wade Ward Clawhammer Master book.

34

Ducks on The Millpond

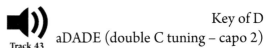

Key of D
aDADE (double C tuning – capo 2)

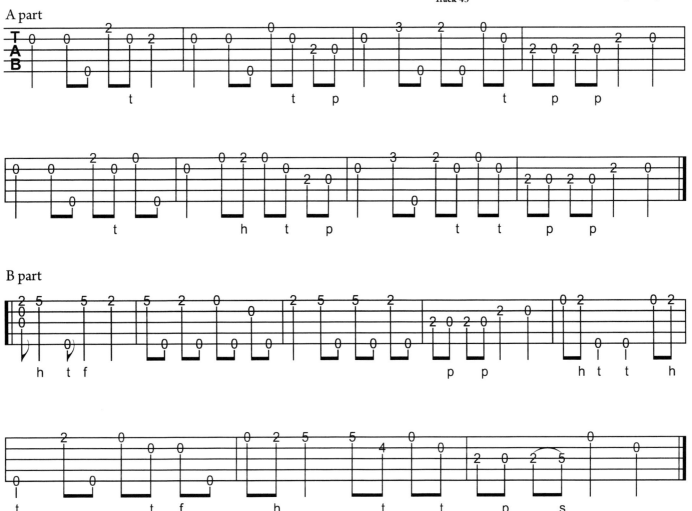

This is another old time jam session classic!

I've written this one out full length instead of two short parts repeated. This way I can give you some more variations. Line 1 and 2 are the same melody which means you could interchange say the first measure of one line for the first measure of the line two. Or mix and match. You can play line 1 two times instead of doing line 2, or two lines of line 2. You get to choose. Have some fun with it and remember as long as you have the core of the tune, this paper is only a guide.

Here's a few words folks often shout out to go with the A part.

Ducks in the mill pond
Geese in the ocean
Hug them pretty gals
If I get the notion

Ducks in the millpond,
Geese in the clover
Tell them pretty girls
I'm comin' over.

Modal Tuning

There are actually many many different tunings that are used in old time banjo playing. Some are even named for the particular tune they are used for, such as *Reuben* tuning or *Sandy River Belle* tuning. And, while most tunes are played in the four major keys of A, C, D and G, those four keys are all covered by the 2 relative tunings we have done so far – G–gDGBD which capoed up is A–aEAC#E and C (or double C as we call it)–gCGCD which capoed up is double D–aDADE.

There is one other popular tuning I want to cover in this book. Most folks call it *Modal tuning*. Since there are actually 7 modes (the major keys we have been playing in so far are actually in the *Ionian* mode for those who are askin'), this name is a bit of a misnomer. Modes actually are about the intervals between the notes. (For a great description of this topic I would refer you to the web page *A la Modes* – http://mmcconeghy.com/RIMUSIC/modesalamode.htm – written in 2006 by Matt McConeghy. Or you can look it up in most music theory texts or The New Harvard Dictionary of Music and read the 3 full pages of tiny text there). Don't worry, I don't fully understand it either. It makes my head hurt too!

SO, we are going to retune our banjo to play in the *Dorian* mode, which has a flatted third and seventh notes in the scale. (PHEW, ENOUGH of that.) This is often referred to as *mountain minor* or *sawmill* tuning. We will just call it *modal*. We are going to retune the notes to gDGCD for G modal which becomes A model (aEADE) when we capo up two frets. The good news is that we only have to retune one string! Your *fourth* string. Lets go step by step.

First take your capo off (yes, fifth string as well) which puts you in double C (gCGCD).

Next, tune your fourth string up one full step from C to D for G modal (gDGCD). Your banjo should now match these pitches for G modal.

Track 44

Here's a scale in G modal.

Track 45

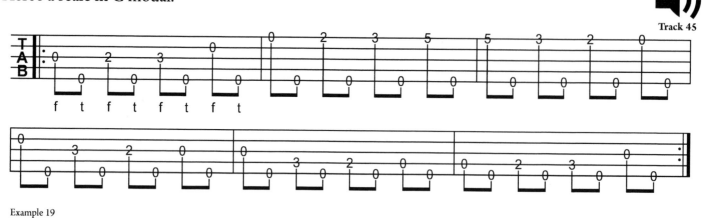

Example 19

Now, put your capo back at the second fret for A modal (aEADE) for one final tune!

Shady Grove

This tune is one of the most popular tunes in A modal.

Shady Grove

Track 46

Key of A - Modal
aEADE (G modal – capo 2)

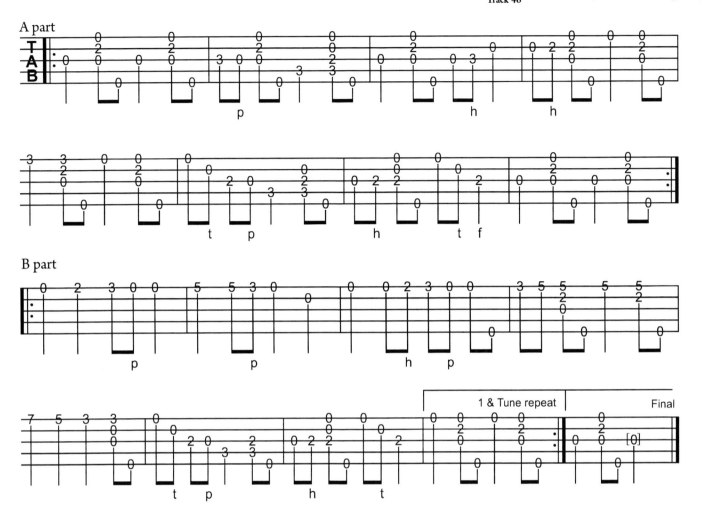

Give yourselves a big hand! You've done it!

Thanks for taking this time with me. I do hope you have enjoyed this journey through your *First Lessons Clawhammer Banjo*. I urge you to listen to as much of this music as you can find. Get it into your head. *Listen, listen, listen.* For more tunes like the ones here, please check out my *Old Time Festival Tunes for Clawhammer Banjo* with over 100 tunes that are popular in the old time scene today. I look forward to working further with you as you continue your journey. Remember, listen to lots of music – espically the old time masters that have come before you, work to be the best you can and play with others. Most importantly:

Play Nice!

Dan *Clawdan* Levenson

Other products by Dan Levenson

Wade Ward - Clawhammer Master - Banjo tablature with companion CD (MB 22243 BCD) Tunes of clawhammer master Wade Ward co-written with Bob Carlin. Two tabs of each of 28 tunes both as the master played them and as they are often interpreted today.

Kyle Creed - Clawhammer Master - Banjo tablature with companion CD (MB 22137 BCD) Tunes of clawhammer master Wade Ward co-written with Bob Carlin. Two tabs of each of 28 tunes both as the master played them and as they are often interpreted today.

Old Time Festival Tunes for Fiddle & Mandolin - Tablature with Standard Notation and 2 companion CDs - Mel Bay Publications (MB 20313 BCD) 117 Old Time favorites with basic and advanced standard notation plus a tab line for mandolin and fiddle.

Gospel Tunes for Clawhammer Banjo - Tablature with Standard Notation and companion CD - Mel Bay Publications (MB 21432 BCD) - 27 Favorite Gospel tunes and hymns in an easy to play format.

Old Time Festival Tunes for Clawhammer Banjo - Tablature with Standard Notation and 2 companion CDs - Mel Bay Publications (MB 20313 BCD) 117 Old Time favorites with basic and advanced tab plus a standard notation line for other instruments.

Clawhammer Banjo From Scratch - Mel Bay Publications (MB 20190BCD) - This book starts at the beginning. 12 common jam session tunes are presented in double thumb and drop thumb technique in Double D tuning. Includes 2 CDs.

Clawhammer Banjo From Scratch - DVD set - Mel Bay Publications -(MB 5003 DVD) - Clawhammer banjo players, start here! This instructional video teaches the basics "From Scratch" through the double thumb Spotted Pony in double C. Disc 2 Tunes you up to Double D and then picks up and adds drop thumb, hammer-ons, pull-offs, more.

Buzzard Banjo Clawhammer Style - Mel Bay Publications (MB 99126BCD) - Tab book with companion CD. 25 tunes tabbed out as played by Dan Levenson with companion CD of the tabs. Includes some basic instruction.

Traveling Home (Buzzard 2005 CD) - Banjo, fiddle, guitar and song solos and duos with Dan, Miss Jennifer and Rick Barron. Tunes: *Red Haired Boy; Leaving Home; John Brown's Dream; Dry & Dusty; Camp Chase/Jenny Git Around; Texas Gals; John Lover's Gone; Texas; Milwaukee Blues; Kentucky John Henry; Lost Indian; Boatman; Durang's Hornpipe; Monkey on a Dogcart; Whistling Rufus; Sandy Boys; Arkansas Traveler/Mississippi Sawyer/Rock the Cradle Joe; Banjo Tramp.*

Barenaked Banjos (Buzzard 2002 CD) - 24 all solo banjo pieces. 4 different banjos! Tunes: *Katy Hill; Logan County Blues; Little Billie Wilson; Dr. Dr.; Texas Gals; Forked Deer; Staten Island; Liza Poor Gal; Johnny Don't Get Drunk; Rocky Pallet; Needlecase; Old Bell Cow; Fortune; Old Molly Hare/Rag Time Annie; Soldier's Joy; Billy in the Low Ground; Joke on the Puppy; Breaking Up Christmas; Whiskey Before Breakfast; Hangman's Reel; Duck River; Flying Indian; June Apple; Wild Horses at Stoney Point.*

Light of the Moon (Buzzard 2001 CD) - Fiddle tunes to folk songs are what you will find in this recording. Dan is joined on a few songs with other musicians including Annie Trimble of the Boiled Buzzards, and his son Jonathan. Tunes: *June Apple; Cindy; Rushing the Pepper; Climbing the Golden Stairs; All God's Critters; Jaybird/Moses Hoe the Corn; Old Rip; The Fox; Rockin' Jenny; Soppin' the Gravy; Willow Waltz; Darlin' Corey; Buffalo Gals; Yellow Rose of Texas; Shelvin' Rock/Old Mother Flanagan; Snake River Reel; Hard Traveling; John Stenson's #2; Roseville Fair; Front Porch Waltz.*

New Frontier (Blue rose 1001 CD) - All instrumentals w/Dan Levenson on banjo, fiddle and guitar and Kim Murley on hammered dulcimer and Yang Qin (Chinese hammered dulcimer). Tunes: *Kitchen Girl/Growling Old Man, Grumbling Old Woman; Weaving Girl; Lullaby; Pachinko; Liza Poor Gal/Traveling Down the Road; Dance of the Yao People; Red Haired Boy; Duke of Kent's Waltz; Thunder on a Dry Day; Horse Race; Flying Indian; Dragon Boat; Mackinac Bats; Rosy Cloud Follows the Moon; Song of the Frontier; Cherry Blossom Waltz.*

Early Bird Special (Buzzard 1004 CD) - Dan plays with The Boiled Buzzards Old Time Stringband. Tunes: *Smith's Reel; Beasties in the Sugar; Wooden Nickel; Brandywine/Three Forks of Reedy; The Engineers Don't Wave From the Train Anymore; Black Widow Romp; Young Guns and Miners; Boys Them Buzzards Are Flying; Lulu Loves Them Young; Bitter Creek; Lost Everything; Nixon's Farewell; Teabag Blues; Sadie at the Back Door/Waiting for Nancy; You Can't Get There From Here; Snake River Reel; Grey Haired Dancing Girl; Cliff's Waltz.* Mostly instrumental (vocals on 2 cuts) banjo, fiddle, guitar, and acoustic bass.

Eat at Joe's (Buzzard 1003 CD) - Dan plays with the Boiled Buzzards. Tunes: *Paddy on the Turnpike; John Brown's March/Waiting for the Federals; Snake River Reel; Hollow Poplar; Spotted Pony; Dinah/Wake Up Susan; Black Widow Romp; Katy Hill; Nixon's Farewell; Shady Grove; Spring in the Valley; Cuffy; The Year of Jubilo/Yellow Rose of Texas; Jimmy in the Swamp; Nixon's Farewell (w/double fiddles); Julianne Johnson; Tombigbee Waltz.* All instrumental music played on banjo, fiddle, guitar, and acoustic bass.

Fine Dining (Buzzard 1002 CD) - Dan plays with the Boiled Buzzards. Tunes: *Shuffle About; Little Dutch Girl; John Brown's Dream; Liza Jane; Goodbye Miss Liza; Booth Shot Lincoln; Briarpicker Brown; Monkey on a Dogcart; Fortune; Shenandoah Falls; Three Ponies; Jaybird; Forked Deer/Doctor Doctor; Leaving Home; Rock the Cradle Joe; Old Mother Flanagan; Santa Claus; Too Young to Marry; Roscoe; Stambaugh Waltz.* Mostly instrumental (vocals on 2 cuts) banjo, harmonica, guitar, and acoustic bass.

Salt and Grease (Buzzard 1001 CD) - is The Boiled Buzzards' first album. Tunes: *Julianne Johnson; 3 Thin Dimes; Durang's Hornpipe; Milwaukee Blues; Muddy Roads; Log Chain/Railroading Across the Rocky Mountains (Marmaduke's Hornpipe); Billy in the Lowground; Yellow Barber; Little Billy Wilson; Sandy Boys; Southtown; Rochester Schottische; Kansas City Reel; June Apple; Bull at the Wagon; Sally Ann Johnson; Nail That Catfish to a Tree; Icy Mountain; Benton's Dream; Sadie's Waltz.* Mostly instrumental (vocals on 2 cuts) banjo, harmonica, guitar, and acoustic bass.

**For more information and to order Dan's products,
please go to www.Clawdan.com**

Dan Levenson is a Southern Appalachian native who has grown up with the music of that region. Today he is considered a respected master teacher and performer of both the Clawhammer banjo & Appalachian style fiddle.

Dan has won awards on both instruments including first place at the 2005 Ohio Clawhammer Banjo Championship and Grand Champion at the 2010 Ajo, AZ fiddle contest. He has over 10 recordings both with his band The Boiled Buzzards and as a solo artist.

Dan performs and teaches regularly throughout the country. He has taught at many of the traditional music schools and camps including the John C. Campbell Folk School, Mars Hill, Maryland Banjo Academy, The Ozark Folk Center at Mountain View, AR and Banjo Camp North. He currently also runs various clawhammer banjo, fiddle and stringband workshops as well as his innovative *Clawcamp* throughout the year.

Dan is the Mel Bay author of *Clawhammer Banjo From Scratch, Buzzard Banjo Clawhammer Style, Old Time Festival Tunes for Clawhammer Banjo, Old Time Festival Tunes for Fiddle & Mandolin, Gospel Tunes for Clawhammer Banjo, Kyle Creed Clawhammer Banjo Master* and *Wade Ward Clawhammer Banjo Master*. He writes for *The Old Time Herald* and is a writer and editor for *Banjo Newsletter's Old Time Way*.

**For Dan's books, recordings and more information about Dan
please go to www.Clawdan.com**